Twenty Years to Run a Mile

By

Alyssa Marie

"A new and talented poet and writer. Fresh words capture moments, memories, and milestones. Her poems capture the sentiments we all share about family, friendship, love, and loss."

—MJ Nightingale

<u>Table of Contents</u>

Author's Note

I do not take pleasure in meaningless words. I cannot be soothed by lies and I will not write them. All that you are about to read is true...in one way or another. Every poem is deeply personal—a penned segment of my heart. I have written to a time that's passed; I have written to the ones I've loved and lost, and to those who will never know of the ink I've spilled for them; I have written to myself and to you, dear reader. In doing so, I have bled and I have healed and I am now prepared to do it all again if ever I must.

While the pages turn, I would like you to remember a few things: The love you felt was real...even if they did not love you back; the times that you miss *did* happen, even if the memories are blurred; the people who are gone have found a way to stay with you; you are *strong*. Do not be discouraged. We are *all* just wolves without names until we decide on why we roam. It took me twenty years to run this first mile.

Part 1
The part I had to write down before I could forget...

Little, Big Things

Pistachio ice-cream with chocolate
crunchies…
Knowing that great-grandma liked it the same.

Peanut butter and Nutella…

Folgers coffee
and the smell of hair dye…

Overly protective fire alarms,
cigarette butts in the garden patch
and boiled pasta on the floor.
I come from my grandfather's stories of love,
life, and war.

The Belmont horses.
"Aaanndd they're off!"

Road trips.
"Just because."
Good times…
better music.

A large table that can never fit everybody.
Faith and wisdom.

Memories of the long-gone.
Hopes for the far away.

I come from the crazy and the loud.
I come from late nights,
small fights,
and never-ending rewrites.
I come from a dead-end street.

Big Glass Cases

I remember our three-bedroom apartment.
I remember the small kitchen
and the soft pink of my room.
I remember walking through the dark hallway
at night
to sneak in between my parents.

Our three-bedroom apartment—
where only four people lived,
but where many people stayed.

I remember the pigeon that made a nest
and laid eggs on our balcony.
We fed her grains of rice.

I remember bubble baths,
and elevators,
and putting quarters into the washer machine.

I remember running around the house
with my brother
looking for my father
who was hiding under the bed all along.

My mom would caution us about the
neighbors
because of all the noise that we were making.
My dad would kiss her and tell her not to
worry.

Now we live in a house.
It's much bigger than what we had,
but there's no room for a pigeon.
There's nowhere to run.
The table is set for three.

Things are good.
They're just not like they were.
We tried for more than we had
and wound up with less, it seems.
There is no elevator to go up and down in.
The water falls straight down the drain.
I no longer make trips down a dark hallway.

I remember the family we used to be
in our three-bedroom apartment.

The Curse the Witch Made

The witch boiled water in her big black pot.
"Could I have thought a better curse? No, I could not!"

She paced around the room and looked through her drawers.
"This brew will hold power! It'll start and end wars!"

She looked at her crow, the one she named 'Theft'.
"Ah, yes! Black feathers for death!"

The crow stared at her, his eyes narrowed thin.
"Well, I'll throw in some sunshine! Just pass me the gin!"

So she added the sunshine, the gin, and the feather.
"Oh, this is good, but I'll make it much better!"

She pulled out some eyeballs, some lips, and a heart.

"I'll mix in some fun that'll last through the start!"

Some sprinklings of loneliness, but only a few.
"Passion! Attraction! That, we'll need too!"

Who else but she could have made such a trick?
"I must add more flour! It's not quite yet thick."

The crow perched on her shoulder then tugged on her hair.
"Oh, what do you want? Fine, I'll put in some care!"

She threw in two teardrops—one happy, one sad.
"I wonder, Theft, if it's good or it's bad…"

rain don't hurt

go on.
stand outside.
so what 'it's wet'?
wet couldn't kill ya!
it only looks ugly through the window…
if you'd try it, you'd know.
to stand outside
with your arms held out,
eyes closed…
feels like freedom.
'too wet'.
hmph.
eh, you kids today.
ya don't know what's good for ya.

What is Poetry?

Poetry.
The *beauty*
found in chaos.

Poetry.
The *love*
found in hurt.

Poetry.
The *tears*
seen through your smile.

Poetry.
All those
unspoken words.

Razors Without Blades

"I think I need a shave,"
he told me,
reaching for the Barbasol.

I smeared a white cloud of foam around his
face,
then took some more down his neck.

"Might as well get my arms,"
he said,
handing me the razor.

I slid it slowly across his cheek,
afraid that I might cut him.
He only smiled, his eyes dark green
and examined himself in the mirror.

"Ah, that's a good shave,"
he said to me
and we went about our playing.

Little did I know
that the blade was in his hand
all along.

Grilled-cheese Smile Days

I may love all these
License-having-boyfriend-kissing-walking-
in-the-street days
but, God, I miss those
Bubble-blowing-seesaw-singing-dancing-
feet-on-feet days!

And every time I live another
Driving-by-myself day
I think of all the
Backseat-riding-grilled-cheese-smiling-
cannot-reach-the-shelf days!

It's great to have these
Poem-writing-money-making-should-not-hit-
the-snooze days
but if I could, I'd go back to those
"Help-me-tie-my-shoes" days!

Little Girls with Long Black Curls

I heard there are two little girls
as cute as they could be,
who hopped aboard a pirate ship
and sailed across the sea.

They like to dance, and run, and skip,
and shake their long black curls.
They each wear crowns atop their heads
made new from gold and pearls.

Every day they laugh and play
and dance their twisty twirls.
Oh, how I wish to board that ship
with those two little girls.

Whistle Through Rain

I walk with my cane
while I'm out in the rain
and sing to the sky while it cries.

I met a boy on my way
to the following day
who told unbelievable lies.

He whispered a whisper
as thin as a whisker.
He said, "old men never die."

"They only sing songs
because they lived long.
There's so much they're leaving behind."

I tapped on my cane,
still whistling through rain
and waited to hear him say why.

He said "Only old men with canes
will whistle through rain
and sing to the sky while it cries."

Part 2
The part I wrote while half empty…

After the Funeral

I wish today was yesterday
or maybe the day before.
I wish today was not today
so I could see your face once more.

Dancing Feet On Feet

"Silent Night," the angel sang,
I remembered as the church bells rang.

The song was short, but our dance was long
so we had it on repeat.
Those were the days when we were together,
dancing feet on feet.

Our "la la las" rang in my ears
but I wouldn't let them bring me tears.

Though times passed by,
the angel won't sing,
and these memories are bittersweet,
I'll remember the days when we were
together,
dancing feet on feet.

Race Day at Belmont

The sun is looking bright today.
I'm sure that you can see.
But I wouldn't mind the rainy days
if you were here with me.

You Told Her Not To Cry

My how she cried.
But she didn't want to cry.

You told her not to cry.
You said you would come back.
You said it would be quick.
And you told her not to cry.

But, God, how she cried
though she didn't want to cry.

Turkey on Rye

Sometimes I sit at the kitchen table
and wonder if you're flying high.
I sit and think of the days
when we ate turkey on rye.

Sometimes I sit at the kitchen table
when there is not much else to do,
then find it doesn't feel right at the table
not sitting next to you.

I think of the days we would sit there and
laugh.
You'd unwrap your sandwich
then offer me half.

Now, I go up to the butcher,
he asks, "what would you like to buy?"
I smile small to myself and say,
"I'd like turkey on rye."

My Favorite Valentine

We all have one love
who has stood the test of time.
Oh, Pop! How is heaven?
Oh, sweet Valentine of mine.

I don't want you to worry
if I find somebody new.
Even if he makes me laugh
the same way you used to do.

He can buy me all the chocolates
and choose the very best card to sign.
He can write words sweet as honey
and somehow make them rhyme.

But you soothed every heartache.
Oh, the mountains you would climb.
All my life, you'll always be
my favorite Valentine.

Endings

I walk the graveyard of my life
and mourn the past
buried beneath my feet.
My eyes are wet
as I scan the tombstones
of the memories
I've forgotten,
the ones I've pushed aside,
and the ones I wish could hold my hand.

Part 3

The part I wrote while lost and awkward…

The Wolf Without a Name

The Fox watched from his hole.
He'd heard legends about this beast—
the foul looking creature
who roamed the woods alone
where the trees don't sprout flowers
and the wind blew only cold.

Born a runt, cast aside, and now the largest of
them all.
Every night he comes outside to sing a
tortured call.

The Fox had known that he was near.
He'd heard the breathy sighs,
he'd felt the ground tremble with the weight
of heavy paws,
he'd stuck his head out of the snow to try and
catch a glimpse
of the drifter of these woods, who had a title
but not a name.

His eyes were marbled storm clouds
that could pierce right through your soul.
He had long and shaggy fur that was matted
to his skin,

his claws were blades of iron
that scraped against the ground.

He walked slow and patiently,
knowing he wouldn't be bothered.
But it wasn't until he smelled him
that the beast peered through the snow
and stared at the tiny creature
who was watching from afar.

The Fox's body shivered.
He thought he'd be a snack,
but instead of coming after him,
the beast just turned back.

He'd gone back to his drifting,
he walked the night alone,
and all that's left to show for it
are his prints that mark the snow.

The Fox knew he shouldn't.
He should have gone back in his hole,
but he found he was too curious
to leave legends alone.
He followed slowly and quietly,
and stayed low to the ground.

The beast had known that he'd been
followed,
but he merely sauntered on.
He ignored the tiny footsteps
and prepared to sing his song.

He knew the legend built around him,
he simply didn't care.
It didn't matter what others thought,
he'd live his life the same.
It made for peaceful living,
to be a wolf without a name.

The Star's Black Sky

What am I hungry for?

That's a hard question for me to answer.
I never really ask for much.
I try not to expect much either.
But there *is* something I want.
Whatever that *something* may be.

Did you ever miss something like the stars
would miss a black sky?
Did you ever find yourself unable to pinpoint
what it was you were missing?

That's how I feel most days.
I read somewhere once that we will always be
hungry—
that there will always be that little bit of
emptiness.

What is your black sky?

I'm not sure what mine is.
Sometimes I think I will never find out.
For now, I think I only want what I have
given.

After that, we'll see.
Maybe then I will be full.

But What of the Moon?

So many love the Sun.
They think it *kind*
for the light that it brings.
No one hates it
for the burns on their backs
or the sweat on their brows.

But what of the moon?

The Sun—cruel and unfeeling
in its glory,
lost
in its arrogant brightness,
will part clouds
and frame its beauty with rainbows.

It will rise with great strength
and set with much grace
and all will pray
for dawn the next day.

But what of the moon?

The moon will shine a light
on those the Sun gave up on.

The moon will share the night
with the stars.

Hostess

Here comes:
Wednesday!
Sucky Wednesday.
Weekly-*worst-day* Wednesday.
Bitchy-people-Wednesday...
Kill me.

Running

We're always running.
Out of breath,
out of time.
We run to love
and away from it.

We run our fingers through our hair
to try
and untangle the mess
that we are.

We let water run over our heads
and think that
maybe
it will wash away
the pains of yesterday.

Blood runs through our veins
and connects us
to people
and places.

We run our *every*
next step
by other people.

We run into
ourselves
and other obstacles.

We run out
of words to say.
Out of excuses.
Out of reasons to stay upset.

I run a constant race.

Running.
Always running.

Anti-Ode to Friendship: "A Toast to My Friend"

Here's to the time we've spent together
and the things I've done for you.
Here's to the effort you don't put in.
and the things you'd never do.

Here's to the 'same old' that's gone sour
and the excuses that you make.
Here's to all the hurt I've told you
to the concern you seem to fake.

Here's to the things we said we'd do
and to the times that you "forgot"
Here's to *your* shorthand answers
and to you asking for *my* lot.

Here's to the messages you don't answer
and to the ones that you don't send.
Here's to the love that's unrequited.
Here's to the one I call my friend.

Puddles Like Us

Puddles.

I hate you.
I hate you!
I *hate* you!

I do!

No.
Not really.
Not when it's raining.

Not when I'm twirling
and barefoot
and calm.

I hate you when the sun is shining
and I'm wearing sandals
and I find you under my feet.

Somehow, I never walk away feeling dry.
There's always anger,
happiness,
sadness,
or something else.

October 25th

I'm struggling to write.

So I'll write about how I can't write.

I'll write about how I lie awake
trying to find the words
but the words
won't
come.

I'll write about how
passions
are *fragile*
and about how
existence
is *exhausting*.

I'll write about how
they stole the pen from my hand
right before they threw my body
      into
           the
               sea.

Not Today.

I can't do it.
Not today.

All they do is complain about what they can't
change
and ignore the things that should be changed.
AND forget to buy eggs.
AND dump my unfinished coffee.
All they do is say things they don't mean
and make promises they can't keep.

They do things like *die*.
They do things like leave.

So many hypocrites.
So many chauvinists
So many opinions I'm expected to care about.

And I *just* want to read.
Can you *just* let me read?

God, it's always so nice until humans show
up.

All they do is cry for the life that they want

and do *nothing*.
AND they chew with their mouths open.
AND they cough on the back of my neck.
All they do is break the hearts that were given
to them.

How 'bout those who bring up the past?
Go on.
Repeat the same thing over and over.
No one's sick of you.
We're all still listening.

Why do I stay alone?

Ever dealt with kids?
They're snotty little brats.
Ever worked with adults?
Such arrogant jerks.

The miserable are happy to be miserable.
The haters are haters because they were
hated.
The ones who love are not always loved.

And so, we're left with…
hypocrites,
and chauvinists,
and empty coffee cups.

We're left with…

Damn!
Which one of you
assholes ate the last of
the Oreos?!

No.
I'm sorry.
I just can't do any peopling today.

The Gifts of Time

Time will bring you hurt,
Time will bring you failure,
Time will bring you reasons to leave
and slowly lessen the reasons to stay.
Time will bring you death…
So much death.
But the worst cruelty is that
                time
will bring you love to accompany it all.

The Wolf Who Loved The Moon

Not many knew his story
or the reason for his song.
He'd heard the many rumors,
all of them were wrong.

He'd wandered through the nights,
that much I know is true.
But nothing's black and white
and I won't be the fool.

He was a wolf with many secrets.
That just never changed.
That said, there are many legends
built around his name.

"Beast" was what they called him.
A result of his massive size,
and his howling in the night:
his song sang for the sky.

He never cared for company.
Not that he had the option.
The others stayed away
and kept to the precaution.

He had a look about him.
So many thought him cruel.
But he was just a wolf.
A wolf who loved the moon.

He soon got to his cave
and looked up at the sky.
He'd waited the whole day
for the sun to pass him by.

He waited for the clouds to part
and then he saw the moon.
He took a deep breath in
and sang his rapture tune.

This, I believe, is what they called "the
tortured cry".
It didn't sound like other songs,
that much I can't deny.

But there he was, every night,
to sing his doting hymn.
For the moon was the only one, you know,
who had seen the heart within.

They were quite the pair, you see.
He gave, and she gave back.
They both had broken pieces.

Together, they filled gaps.

She lived in the dark,
but brought light into his world.
Nothing that much different
from a boy who loves his girl.

He suffered much sadness,
but his songs…
they brought her joy.
Isn't that the same as a girl who loves her
boy?

And now here we are.
You've come to see the truth.
The one you thought to be a beast,
was just a wolf who loved the moon.

Part 4
The part I wrote with an ache in my chest…

Tails in the Dark

We're wary of devils.
We never fear saints.
We ignore the images
and marvel the paints.
Understand that truths
can often be stark.
For even saints
could have tails
in the dark.

Before the Good Gets Too Lazy

I tend to find my words
after all things fall apart.
But where are all my writings
for the not yet broken heart?

I'd like to speak in present terms
before the light goes dim.
So I'll quickly write a poem for you,
while aware my odds are slim.

I'll write about hope.
I'll write about maybe.
I'll write about the good
before the good gets too lazy.

It's possible I'll find a tail,
or learn you're made of dirt and grime
but you're standing there,
across the room,
and from here you look just fine.

The Could Have Been That Never Was

I don't know why your heart went cold,
or when the weather changed.
I don't know how the taste went sour,
or if our *something* gets a name.

But I think of how I felt with you,
and there are things I *hope* you know.
I'll only say them once.
Then after, I'll let go.

Our something may have been nothing
and had the briefest hold on time,
but it was real,
it was good,
and if it wasn't ours…
it was mine.

The Poem that Failed

I was staring at the moon last night,
and I thought you'd like it too.

Don't ask me why I thought that,
'cause I'm not really sure.

I'm waiting for these poems to work,
if I'm telling you the truth.

I think about you all the time,
when I'm not thinking of other things.

I don't know when that part will stop,
and I'm not sure what it means.

I think of why I should be mad,
but then I remember why I'm not.

If it wasn't for those eyes of yours...

I'm still waiting for these poems to work
since there's not much else to do.

But I was staring at the moon last night,
and I thought you'd like it too.

New Present Terms

I tend to find great words
after all things fall apart.
There are no better writings
than for the lovely broken heart.

It seems we have new present terms
now that the light's gone dim.
My fault for writing poems to you
while aware my odds were slim.

Forget about hope.
Forget about maybe.
Forget about the good
because it's true that good is lazy.

No, you don't have a tail,
and you're not made of dirt or grime.
But I walked across the room to you,
and from here you look less fine.

A Jingling of Pennies

If I was a lover,
I'd kidnap you.
I'd take the word 'love'
and give it truth.

I'd erase the lies
laced between its letters
that are threaded together
so loosely
and thrown around
so carelessly.

If I was a lover
I'd turn this copper
into gold.
I'd show you the power
of a capable heart.
I'd lasso the moon
and hand you the stars.

Too bad I'm a loner.
So love is just
a jingling of pennies
and an empty black sky.
But if I was a lover,

I'd kidnap you.

I Can't Give You Poetry

I don't want you to change, love.
Don't do anything.

Not
one
thing.

Because I can't give you poetry.

I can give you my time.
I can give you my hand to hold.
I can give you eyes.
I can give you a smile.
But not poetry.

You're not one for poems, love.
I can't confuse brief moments
with what's true.
The ink would bleed
into ill-fated waters.
You'll dive in the deep end
and forget to come up for air.

You're not afraid of drowning, love.
Don't change.

Never change.

I'll stay sober for the both of us.
I might sneak a bit of my heart into your back
pocket.

But I can't give you poetry.

If Ever We Should…

The issue with you and me is that
we're so *impossible*,
so *inevitable*.
It's tragic.

Sometimes I wonder…
What would happen if we gave in?
If ever we should.

I told you once that you weren't afraid of
drowning.
But I was so very wrong.

I think,
you're more afraid of ink
than *anyone* I've ever met.
I think,
what's true is true.
I think,
The confused one, here,
is you.

I won't ask you to change, love.
I already *know* I shouldn't *ever* give you
poetry.

Still,
I know what you're wondering…
If ever we should.
Oh, darling,
let me tell you
what a beautiful poem that would be…

Sunlight Through a Glass Window

My language is poetry.

I speak it in whispers so that my secrets
don't hear their names being called
and so that my stolen moments
won't sense me thinking of them.

For they know my faults,
though I am not to blame.

This is *not* a lament!

Spoken words may destroy
but inky words can redeem.

So I wrote how I am just a woman
in *love* with possibilities.
I do not seek to rob what is not mine.
But in the heat of sunlight through a glass
window,
the world belonged to *me*.

Screw faults.
Screw guilt.
Screw whatever's not yet redeemed.

My language is poetry
and I'll write my way through it!

Remorse be *damned*!

The first time my hand was held,
I knew that poems
—true poems—
are made
and re-written
by moments
like these.

Part 5
The part where I got older…

Ha! Too Little, Ha! Too Late

Now,
is when they want to speak
of hurt
of loneliness
of sorrow.

Now,
they reach for me.
Longing for
a soft touch
a warm embrace
an open heart.

Now,
when the tears have all passed
are they willing to hear me cry.

Now,
after I have stitched
my *own* heart back together,
do they ask me
how badly it hurt
to break.

Truth?

I was considerate.
I was willing.
(And a little bit naive).

They should have come to me
when
they had
the chance.

There was a time
when I cared
to search for love
in empty people
and in hollow spaces.
When I fell for the lies
beneath familiar faces.

Now,
that I have learned to stand my ground
do they wonder if I shake.

Not anymore!

For others,
I have waited.
To others,
I gave welcome.

They did not do the same.

Truth?
I no longer have the time.
I no longer have the room.
I'm doing what's best for *me*.

And
I
do
not
apologize!

My Hair is Curly!

My hair is curly.

For years, I have
pressed it,
tied it,
clipped it,
snipped it,
hidden it…

I've moused it,
gelled it,
"anti-frizzed" it.
I've tried everything
but could not restrict it.

My hair is curly!

It is one big, thick, frizzy mess
given to me by God.

It is mine.
It is beautiful.
And it is friggin' curly!

Hmph!

Remember This!

Forgive my candor when I say,
I do not care who betrayed you.
I do not care who can't love you.
I do not care who hates you.
I do not care who is pressuring you.
I do not care who is still angry
over something you did
when you were sixteen.

Screw them!
They will guilt you.
They will patronize you.
They will belittle you
and *everything* you do.

You will lose yourself in such a crowd.
For they will
hang off your shoulders,
cover your eyes,
and kick you in the ankles.

And when they do,
remember this…
Nobody knows
how hard you work,

how deeply you love,
or how badly you hurt.

Do not leave it
up to the historians.

Nobody
is more equipped
to write *your* story
other than *you*.

Incisive and Decisive

I have been told many times
to keep quiet.
I have endured enough condescension
to last me a lifetime.

Listen closely to what they say.
They will tell you
to wait until you are older,
to wait until you are wiser.

Hell,
they will even tell you
to wait until
you are *taller*.

That is when you will be taken seriously,
they say,
that is when
your voice will matter.

What they do not tell you
is that they will never see you
as old enough
or wise enough

because to them,
you will always be twenty
or thirty
years younger.

So when will the moment come?

For me,
it was the day
I took a tape measure
and realized that
I was as tall as I was ever going to get.

From then on,
I refused to remain content
in my own silence.

So
the next time they told me
to quiet down,
I spoke louder.

The next time it was suggested
that I keep my opinions to myself,
I resolved to be incisive
and decisive.

The next time they advised me

to watch and learn,
I accomplished
and I taught.

The next time I was ordered
to be respectful,
I asked if I, in turn,
would be respected.

I wish you could've seen the look on their
faces.

Battle Tested

I am just an assemblage
of jagged edges.
I cannot feel regret toward
the fire I was forged in
nor the sharpness
of my peaks
nor the heaviness
of my steel.
I have been battle-tested.
I have
and will
do well in war.
I am only sorry
for the ones who believed
I could sit pretty
on a shelf
as home decor.

Solo Act

It's a rush when you take center stage!
Picture this…
You start a monologue
and hope you're saying the words right
but you're never sure
because you can't actually hear yourself
talking
you do the dance number step by step
(well, maybe you miss a few but I don't think
anyone has noticed)
when it's time for the lament
you look down to make sure your feet are on
the box that they drew for you
the light shines hot on you while you perform
the soliloquy
that must have gone well because the
audience applauded at the climax.

Okay, it's halftime
you're out of breath and exhausted
but the curtains open up too quickly
you're not what I would call *ready*
but it's just you up there
and it's *your* show
and it *must* go on

so you sing
and you dance
the sweat drips down your back
your heart can't stop pounding
suddenly
it's time to take a bow.

Wow, that was rough.
Some applaud you.
Some don't.
Some left just before halftime.
I'm not really sure where you got that
bouquet from.
It's pretty, though!
You're tired.

You go home,
have a cookie,
take a shower
then slide into your PJ's.

You put on a good show.
You should be proud.
You'll do it all again
tomorrow…

Let Them Talk

If there's one thing I've noticed
it's that people
do not like
to see you empowered.

If you are proud,
they will call you arrogant.
If you are decisive,
they will call you stubborn.
If you are strong,
they will call you a Bitch.

Don't listen to them.
They are intimidated
by your endurance.
They feel threatened
by your success.
They have convinced themselves
that it somehow makes them
less successful.

And it's sad.
Because I know
you weren't trying to hurt
anyone.
I know

you were only doing
what was best for
you.

It's sad because
those who are trusting
will always be thought fools.
Those in love
will always be thought naive.

If you've managed security
and can take a week off
whenever you want
they will say that you are
lazy.

If you spend your whole life
busting your ass,
they will say
that you are blind
to what is truly important.

Suddenly,
all your virtues
become your folly.

Do what you want.
It's okay.

Let them talk.
You're doing great.

You will *always* be criticized
by the envious people
who wish
deep down
that they were
just
like
you.

Confession

"I am strong."
"I am free."
"I am brave."
"I have healed."

I haven't written enough poems like that.
Not yet.
Because, truly, they are still
just a bunch
of half-truths
strung together
into stanzas.

The truth is
I push myself off the ground
with a tear-stained face
and with shaky knees.

The truth is
my heart has been broken
and is *still* an easy heart to break.

I haven't written enough poems
like the ones you've just read.
If I had,

then I would be
brave enough to love
over and over again.
I would be
strong enough to accept
when love does me wrong.

If I had written enough poems like that,
they would be true
every day
and not just
last Monday.

If I had written enough poems like that,
I would not question
whether I have any right
to write them at all.

The truth is
that I am still learning.
The truth is
those poems are…
not so much reflections
of the person I am…
but reflections
of the person
I am working hard to be.

And my efforts can't possibly be in vain.
As I write this
I realize
that my face
may be stained with tears
but my head is held high.

As I write this
I realize
my knees may be shaking
but I am up, off the ground.

As I write this
I realize
I may be afraid
but I love anyway.
Deeply
and without question.

As I write this
I realize
The stitches on my heart
may have fallen loose
but the needle is in my hand.

So there.
Maybe I have written enough poems like
these after all.

And maybe, I don't have much right to write them…
But they're in here.
Do with them what you like.

Acknowledgments

The part where I say 'thank you!'

Firstly, I should like to thank Oreo cookies for being insanely delicious and for coming in six-packs which are easy to sneak around during writer's hous.

Next, I have to thank my parents for pushing me to be my best and for incessantly asking, "when's the book gonna be done?" Thanks, guys. Sorry for some of the mush that's in here. Who would've thought I'd be such a softy. Yucky, I know.

Of course, I have to thank the rest of my family—my brother, my uncles, my aunts, my cousins, my great uncles and aunts...the whole shebang. I know you all are going to be incredibly embarrassing/supportive and tell everyone you know about this one, and the one after this, and so on. I couldn't ask for better.

Thank you, Abi, for looking over each poem and saying, "yeah, that'll work."

Nikki! Thank you for taking the most beautiful pictures of me! Without you, the cover would not be possible.

Here's to my aunt MJ who continues to be my mentor. I have learned so much from you. Thanks for getting me going and for keeping me laughing.

To my Grandparents! Forever and always. You guys already know. Thanks for the wind in my wings.

I love you all!

Special thanks to Leigh Bardugo who, at a book signing, ensured me that I was a real writer and made me promise that I would finish whatever I was working on. One day she's going to see something of mine. If it happens to be this one, I would want her to know that she's the writer I strive to be.

Lastly, I would like to thank whoever thought it would be worth it to pick up something I've written. It means a lot. YOU mean a lot. I hope you liked it and that it did something for you. Be strong. Have fun. Do great. Walk the extra mile.

(P.S. A couple of these poems would not be possible without the people who inspired them. Thanks anyway. You guys have no idea who you are. That's exactly how I like it.)

XOXO,
Alyssa

About the Author

Alyssa Marie was born and raised in Long Island. She began her writing career as co-author of *The 12th Factor Series* and then published her poetry collection, *Twenty Years to Run a Mile.* Alyssa Marie is currently a student at Long Island University and is studying English Education. Her belief in the importance of literature has influenced her career path and is what has driven her to write.

You can follow Alyssa Marie on:

Instagram: @writer.alyssa.marie

BookBub:
https://www.bookbub.com/profile/alyssa-marie

**For business inquiries, you can contact Alyssa Marie at:
authoralyssamarie@gmail.com**

Also by Alyssa Marie
The 12th Factor: We are the Strong

Decades after a war that tore the country apart, New America is filled with dark secrets hidden behind deceiving smiles and polished shoes. This is the America that Thomas Kent and Regina Banks can't live in any longer—nor can their team of outcasts.

New America is controlled by an elite, mysterious organization with a puppet for a president. They have plans to make America great again and will stop at nothing to make their vision happen. They've also built a wall meant to keep people safe and protect what's theirs. With a sweet-sounding voice on Wolf Radio meant to soothe the masses and make people feel safe, they are taking control over everything. But, living in the shadows of New America are diverse people with remarkable talents, and abilities. The oligarchy in power wants them permanently behind their borders, silenced, or destroyed.

Despite all this, 9 remarkable teenagers vow to live in the shadows no longer, and unveil the truth that is the 12th Factor. But, will anybody listen? Will others join the fight?

Upcoming Projects

The 12th Factor: Backs Against the Wall

Coming 2021/2022

The 12th Factor: End of the Line

Coming 2022/2023